W9-AJO-767

SWAT
TEAM MEMBER

BY PATRICK PERISH

Are you ready to take it to the extreme?
Torque books thrust you into the action-packed world
of sports, vehicles, mystery, and adventure. These books
may include dirt, smoke, fire, and dangerous stunts.
WARNING: read at your own risk.

Library of Congress Cataloging-in-Publication Data

Perish, Patrick.
  SWAT Team Member / by Patrick Perish.
     pages cm. -- (Torque. Dangerous Jobs)
  Includes bibliographical references and index.
  Summary: "Engaging images accompany information about SWAT team members. The combination of
high-interest subject matter and light text is intended for students in grades 3 through 7"-- Provided by
publisher.
  Audience: Ages 7-12.
  ISBN 978-1-62617-198-5 (hardcover : alk. paper)
  1. Police--Special weapons and tactics units--Juvenile literature. 2. Police training--Juvenile literature.
I. Title.
  HV8080.S64P47 2015
  363.2'3--dc23
                                     2014035195

This edition first published in 2015 by Bellwether Media, Inc.

Printed in the United States of America, North Mankato, MN.

TABLE OF CONTENTS

CHAPTER 1

HOSTAGE SITUATION!

A gunman has **barricaded** himself inside a house. He has a **hostage**. The police officers at the scene are not trained for such a dangerous situation. They radio for the SWAT team. The team speeds up in an **armored** van. Its members get into position.

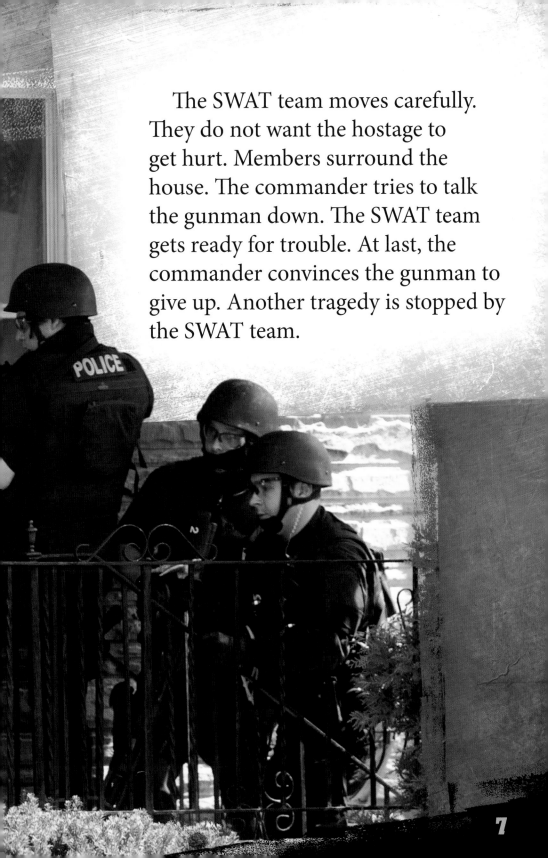

The SWAT team moves carefully. They do not want the hostage to get hurt. Members surround the house. The commander tries to talk the gunman down. The SWAT team gets ready for trouble. At last, the commander convinces the gunman to give up. Another tragedy is stopped by the SWAT team.

CHAPTER 2

SWAT
TEAM MEMBERS

SWAT team members are skilled police officers. SWAT stands for "Special Weapons and **Tactics**." SWAT teams are specially trained for the most dangerous situations. These include hostage situations and **riots**. Teams also provide security for famous people. They protect them from **snipers** or other attacks.

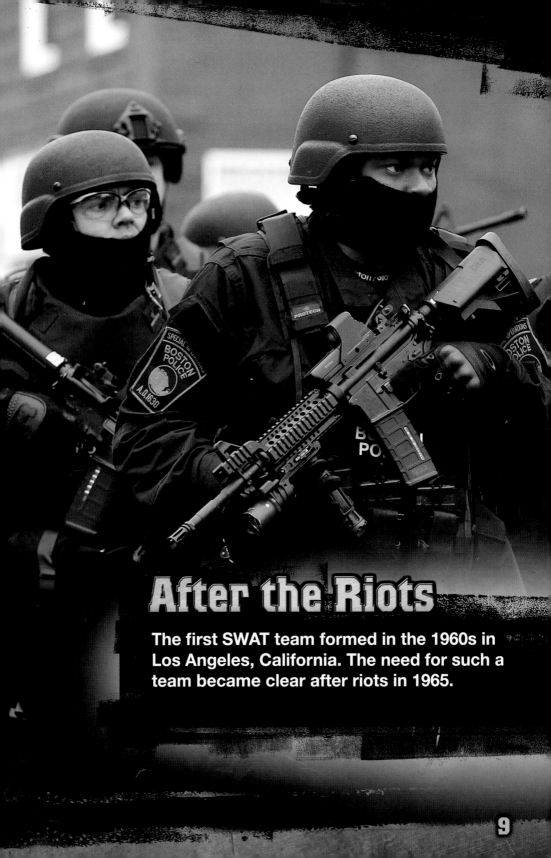

After the Riots

The first SWAT team formed in the 1960s in Los Angeles, California. The need for such a team became clear after riots in 1965.

Becoming a SWAT team member is hard work. Many officers study **criminal justice** in school. Then they need to pass tough fitness tests and written exams. Officers usually need to complete three years of police work after training at the **academy**. Only the best officers are picked to join a SWAT team.

Training never stops for SWAT team members. They practice regularly with their weapons and gear. They use **simulations** to experience dangerous situations.

Fighting Fit

SWAT teams run long distances in heavy body armor. They do push-ups, sit-ups, and other strength tests.

SWAT team members have special gear and powerful weapons. They use **stun grenades** to surprise criminals. **Tear gas** breaks up **violent** crowds.

Lasers let members aim guns on the move. They use **silencers** to keep the guns quiet. **Night-vision goggles** help them see in the dark.

tear gas

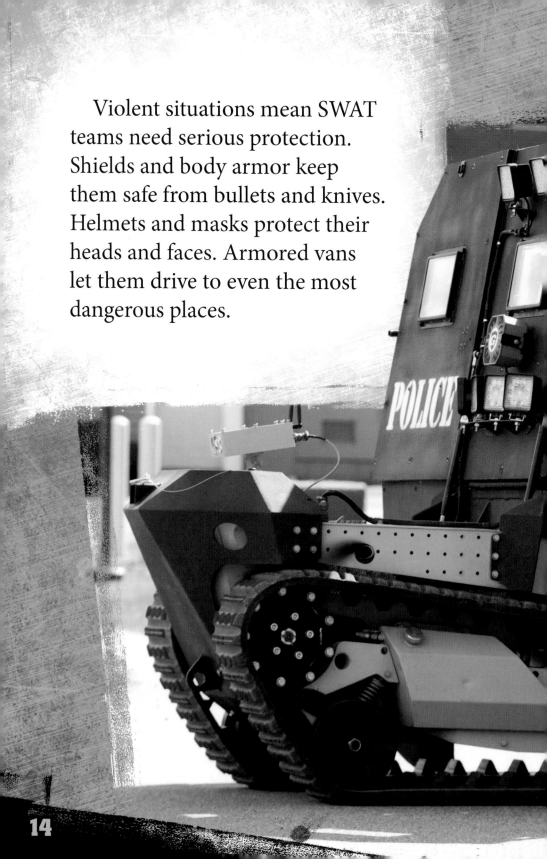

Violent situations mean SWAT teams need serious protection. Shields and body armor keep them safe from bullets and knives. Helmets and masks protect their heads and faces. Armored vans let them drive to even the most dangerous places.

CHAPTER 3

DANGER!

Even with safety gear, SWAT team members face many risks. They often enter buildings without knowing who or what is inside. Gunmen might be hiding from them. Attacks could come from anywhere. Sometimes rooms have bombs or other explosives.

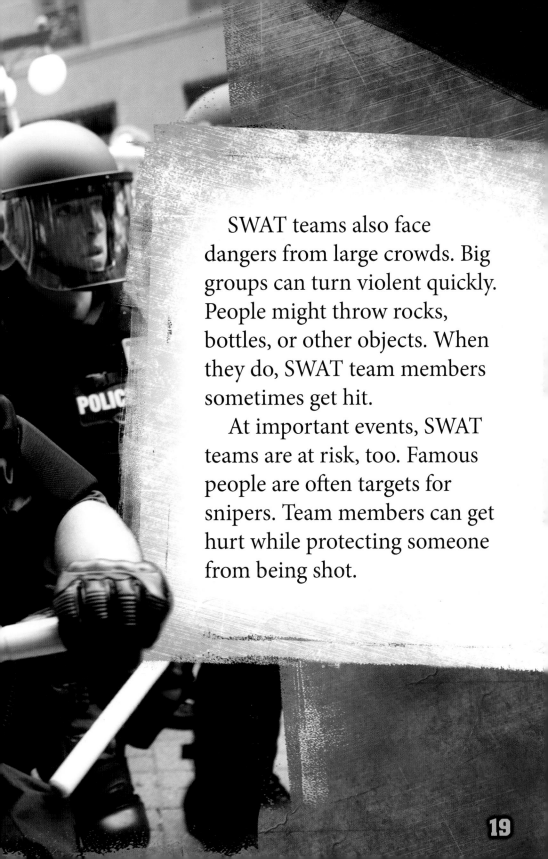

SWAT teams also face dangers from large crowds. Big groups can turn violent quickly. People might throw rocks, bottles, or other objects. When they do, SWAT team members sometimes get hit.

At important events, SWAT teams are at risk, too. Famous people are often targets for snipers. Team members can get hurt while protecting someone from being shot.

SWAT team members are thrown into danger every time they answer a call. They put their lives on the line because they care for their communities. These brave heroes work hard to keep our cities safe.

Tragedy on the Job

On February 7, 2008, SWAT Officer Randal Simmons and his team confronted a gunman in Los Angeles, California. The man had called 911 to report murders he committed. Officer Simmons faced gunfire when he burst into the house. He was taken to a hospital, where he died from his injuries.

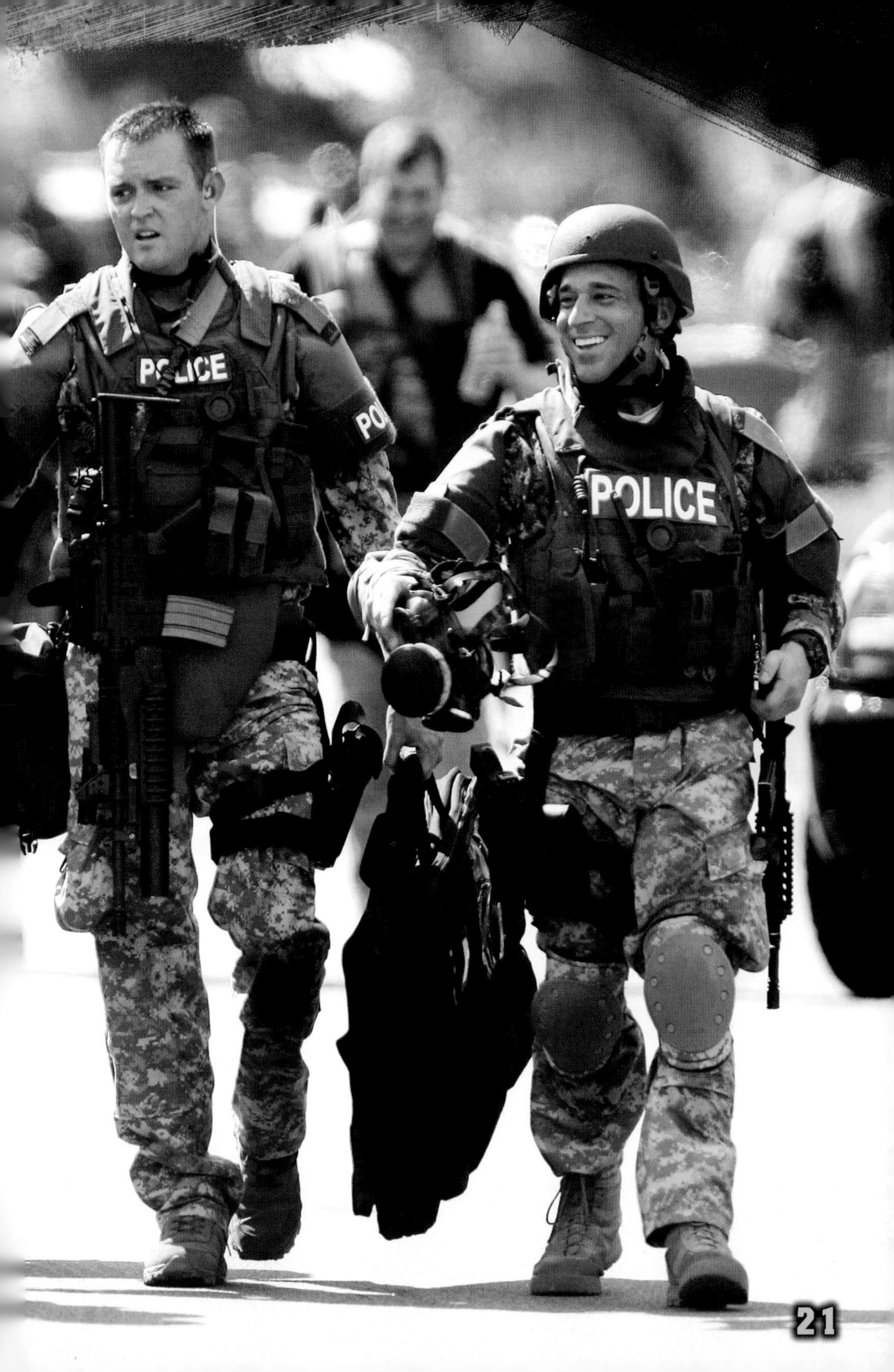
POLICE
POLICE
POLICE

Glossary

academy—the special school where police officers are trained

armored—protected against attacks; armored vehicles have strong metal plates.

barricaded—blocked in

criminal justice—government practices that deal with crime and criminals

hostage—someone held as a prisoner

lasers—beams of light

night-vision goggles—special sets of glasses that allow SWAT team members to see in the dark

riots—gatherings of angry, violent crowds

silencers—devices used to quiet gunfire

simulations—pretend situations that help officers train for emergencies

snipers—long-range shooters

stun grenades—weapons that use bright lights and loud noises to confuse dangerous people

tactics—carefully planned strategies

tear gas—a chemical weapon that irritates the eyes

violent—ready to use harmful physical force

To Learn More

AT THE LIBRARY

Bowman, Chris. *Special Forces Operator.* Minneapolis, Minn.: Bellwether Media, 2014.

Hanson, Anders. *SWAT Team Tools.* Minneapolis, Minn.: ABDO Pub. Company, 2014.

Miller, Connie Colwell. *SWAT Teams: Armed and Ready.* Mankato, Minn.: Capstone Press, 2008.

ON THE WEB

Learning more about SWAT team members is as easy as 1, 2, 3.

1. Go to www.factsurfer.com.

2. Enter "SWAT team members" into the search box.

3. Click the "Surf" button and you will see a list of related web sites.

With factsurfer.com, finding more information

Index